DRINKS AND DESSERTS

CLAUDIA MARTIN

E

Enslow Publishing
101 W. 23rd Street
Suite 240
New York, NY 10011
USA
enslow.com

Published in 2019 by Enslow Publishing, LLC.
101 W. 23rd Street, Suite 240, New York, NY 10011

Editors: Sarah Eason and Jennifer Sanderson
Designers: Paul Myerscough and Simon Borrough
Picture Researcher: Claudia Martin

Cataloging-in-Publication Data
Names: Martin, Claudia.
Title: Drinks and desserts / Claudia Martin.
Description: New York : Enslow Publishing, 2019. | Series: Cooking skills | Includes glossary and index.
Identifiers: ISBN 9781978506640 (pbk.) | ISBN 9781978506374 (library bound) | ISBN 9781978506312 (ebook)
Subjects: LCSH: Beverages—Juvenile literature. | Smoothies (Beverages)—Juvenile literature. | Desserts—Juvenile literature. | Cookbooks—Juvenile literature.
Classification: LCC TX815.M35 2019 | DDC 615.3'99—dc23

Printed in the United States of America

To Our Readers: We have done our best to make sure all website addresses in this book were active and appropriate when we went to press. However, the author and the publisher have no control over and assume no liability for the material available on those websites or on any websites they may link to. Any comments or suggestions can be sent by e-mail to customerservice@enslow.com.

Photo Credits: Cover: Shutterstock: BAMO: bc; choniasub woravichan: br; Luis Echeverri Urrea: bl; Oksana Mizina: tc. Inside: Shutterstock: Africa Studio: pp.10, 11br; Air Images: p.11cr; Alexander Prokopenko: pp.26–27; Alliance: p.19l; Anamaria Mejia: p.35bl; Anastasios71: p.45c; anitasstudio: p.26; Anna_Pustynnikova: p.23l; ArtOfPhotos: p.29t; Artyom Baranov: p.13b; BAMO: p.30; bbernard: p.19r; bernashafo: p.29b; bigjom jom: p.32t; Blend Images: p.21r; bokan: p.11bc; Brent Hofacker: pp.24–25; Color4260: p.9; Cultura Motion p.8; Dean Drobot: p.5; Ekaterina Markelova: pp.44–45; Elena Zajchikova: pp.36–37; Eva Gruendemann: p.17; GLRL: pp.40–41; grafvision: p.13c; Gtranquillity: p.20; Gts: p.15; igorsm8: pp.2–3, 45t, 46–47, 48; iuliia n: pp.42–43, 43t; Jan H Andersen: pp.4–5; Karpenkov Denis: p.33; kkammphoto008: pp.30–31; Konstantin2017: pp.34–35, 36; larik malasha: pp.32–33; Liliya Kandrashevich: pp.20–21; livertoon: pp.38–39; Makistock: p.4; mama mia: pp.12–13; Maridav: p.16; martiapunts: p.31l; Matthew Ennis: p.45b; mimagephotography: pp.1b, 13t; mongione: p.25b; Monkey Business Images: pp.6–7, p.7, p.25t; NAAN: p.38; Nataliya Arzamasova: pp.18–19, 42; Nestor Rizhniak: pp.8–9; Nitr: pp.22–23; Olga Dubravina: p.35cl; Paramonov Alexander: p.32cl; pilipphoto: pp.1t, 14–15, 40; pixelrain: p.27; Rawpixel.com: p.31r; Rido: p.39; Stolyevych Yuliya: p.34; View Apart: p.43b; VikaGeyder: p.37; wavebreakmedia: p.46; Wayhome Studio: pp.28–29; worradirek: p.14; xlibes: p.21l; Yuryev Pavel: p.23r.

CONTENTS

CHAPTER 1
GET COOKING!

Making drinks and desserts is where cooking becomes fun—the recipes may be simple but the results are totally amazing. Roll up your sleeves and get cooking!

A Good Place to Start

The recipes in this book were chosen because they are delicious and will definitely impress your friends and family. On top of that, while you make them, you will be practicing many basic cooking skills, such as chopping and mixing, as well as building a repertoire of more advanced ones, such as folding, crumbling, whisking, and using leavening agents effectively.

Are They Healthy?

These recipes were not chosen for their health benefits! However, when you make your own treats rather than taking them off the shelf in the store, you cut down on unhealthy additives as well as building your awareness of ingredients. You know that a cup of sugar and a block of butter went into that cake! Another good thing is that, having gone to all that effort, you will want to share your masterpieces, helping you stay within healthy-eating guidelines.

Less Is More

These recipes are not intended as a substitute for a healthy diet. A healthy diet contains plenty of vegetables and fruits; low-fat protein such as lean meat, fish, nuts, or beans; low-fat dairy products, such as milk, cheese, or yogurt; and whole grains, such as brown rice or whole wheat bread. The juices in Chapter 1, and many of the other recipes, contain fiber- and nutrient-rich fruit, but fruit also contains natural sugars, so stick to just two portions per day. Many of the recipes also contain saturated fat, found in butter, milk, and other dairy products. Saturated fats are the "bad" fats that can lead to heart disease, so serve your desserts as an occasional treat rather than every day.

Store It Up

As you look through the recipes in this book, you will see that some ingredients appear many times. If you keep these staple ingredients in your pantry or refrigerator, you will be able to rustle up a drink or dessert whenever you feel like it:

- All-purpose flour
- Confectioners' and super-fine sugar
- Cocoa powder or chocolate chips
- Baking powder
- Eggs
- Fresh, dried, and frozen fruit
- Milk or nondairy alternatives
- Ice cream
- Yogurt
- Butter

READ THE RECIPE...

Ready to cook? First of all, choose a recipe you and your friends will enjoy.

Pick a Recipe

Before you choose a recipe, think about who you are serving, the occasion, and how much time you have to prepare your food. For health-focused friends or just for yourself, squeeze up the juices in Chapter 2. For a little more of a treat, turn to the smoothies and shakes in Chapter 3. If you want to cook dessert for a special family meal, flick to the fruity desserts in Chapter 4. If you have some time to spare, turn on the oven for one of the baked goods in Chapter 5. Surprise your friends with a few of the fancy mini desserts in Chapter 6. And finally, for a summer weekend, make some frozen yogurt using the recipes in Chapter 7.

Go to the Store

When you have decided on a recipe, figure out which ingredients you need to buy, and which equipment you need. Most of the recipes serve four people, so multiply or divide as you need. However, the baked goods and mini desserts in Chapters 5 and 6 make a bigger quantity, so keep your leftovers in an airtight container (and the refrigerator if needed) for a few days. When buying your ingredients, remember that some (like flour and sugar) keep for months, while others (like fresh fruit) should be bought just a few days before use.

How Much, How Hot?

In this book, measurements are given in ounces (oz), followed by grams (g), as well as cups, followed by milliliters (ml). There are 240 ml in each cup. Sometimes, you will be told to add a teaspoon (tsp) or tablespoon (tbsp) of an ingredient. There are 5 ml in a teaspoon and 15 ml in a tablespoon. When a "pinch" or a "sprinkle" is suggested, the exact amount is less important—taste as you go to avoid any mishaps.

Oven temperatures are given in Fahrenheit (°F), followed by Celsius (°C). When cooking on a stove, if you do not know how hot to turn the ring, go for a low heat, then turn it up if needed.

Take Over the Kitchen

Always overestimate how long it will take to make your drink or dessert, even when making a simple-sounding juice. Read all the recipe instructions before cracking the eggs. The ingredients are listed in the order they are used, which should help you not to forget anything. If you want to brush up on your cooking skills before you put on your apron, check out the "Mastering the Basics" sections at the start of each chapter.

...OR GO YOUR OWN WAY

You can treat these recipes as guidelines—then switch ingredients in and out.

Try It

The first time you make one of these drinks or desserts, you can play it safe by following the instructions and measuring the ingredients exactly. Then, while you sip your smoothie or pick at your pavlova, ask yourself—and your friends—what is good or not so good about the flavors, textures, and colors. Is the juice too gingery? Are the cranberries too sharp for the froyo? Would you prefer your brownies with the added crunch of peanuts? The "Chef's Tip" box beside each recipe might offer ideas for adding different flavorings. Also check out the "Switch It Up" boxes at the start of each chapter, which offer other ideas for ingredient changes.

Special Diets

If you are vegetarian, or you will be offering your treats to vegetarian friends, all of the recipes are entirely meat- and fish-free. However, if you are vegan, you will need to switch in vegan alternatives for honey, milk, eggs, and other dairy products. Always remember to ask your friends if they have food intolerances and allergies. In particular, remember that nut allergies can be very serious, so think again before adding nuts to those brownies. In the case of a gluten allergy, flours made from other grains, roots, and legumes are often labeled "gluten-free."

Keep It Clean

Before you start to cook or blend, remember these hygiene rules:

- Wash your hands with soap and warm water.
- Make sure all juicers and blenders have been cleaned according to the manufacturer's instructions, and that all other equipment and surfaces are clean.
- If you have long hair, tie it back.
- Wash fruit and vegetables under cold running water, even if you will be peeling them.
- Never serve undercooked eggs, so make sure baked goods are cooked through.
- Check the use-by dates on all ingredients.
- Do not leave dairy products out of the refrigerator for more than two hours.
- Do not refreeze ice cream or frozen yogurt that has melted, and keep the lid on the tub except when serving.
- Refrigerate fresh juices and drink them within one to two days.

CHAPTER 2
JUICES

Juicing is all about extracting the refreshing flavor and nutrients from fruit and vegetables.

What to Juice

If you have an electric juicer or blender, you can turn any fruit into juice, as well as delicious-to-drink vegetables such as carrots, celery, cucumbers, and tomatoes. If you do not have any electric equipment, you can easily juice citrus fruits with nothing more than a knife and a jug. See "Mastering the Basics" for tips on juicing trickier fruits and vegetables by hand.

Drink or Chill

The recipes in this chapter will make four glasses of juice. The best time to drink your juice is immediately after making it. If you do not drink it all at once, put any untouched juice into an airtight container straight after making it and in the refrigerator. It will keep in the refrigerator for one to two days. If the juice separates, just give it a good stir before serving.

Mastering the Basics
Juicing

The easiest and most effective method of juicing is to use an electric juicer, but there are other ways to collect your juice:

1 Electric juicers use drills or blades to chop and squeeze fruits and vegetables. Then they separate the juice from the pulp by spinning, squeezing, and filtering. Unless the fruit and vegetables you are using have edible skin, such as grapes, apples, and cucumbers, peel your produce before juicing. Remember to clean the filter after use.

2 If you have an electric blender, peel your fruits before processing them. Then, to strain out the pulp and seeds, pour the blended mush through a strainer positioned over a bowl.

3 The slowest and least effective method is to juice by hand. Citrus fruits are easily juiced by halving them and squeezing the juice into a jug. Other fruits and vegetables, such as apples and carrots, can be peeled and grated. Put the grated pulp in a cheesecloth, then squeeze it tightly over a bowl.

Switch It Up

The Orange Zinger recipe on page 12 combines oranges with carrots, lemons, and ginger. If you like the healthy, fresh taste of citrus but are not so hot on carrot, try juicing eight oranges with four grapefruits. Or try the delicious combination of six oranges, two limes, and one pineapple.

ORANGE ZINGER

To make four large glasses of this healthy juice, follow this easy recipe.

You Will Need
12 medium carrots
2 medium lemons
8 medium oranges
2-inch (5 cm) piece fresh ginger
Ice to serve

Instructions
1 Trim the ends from the carrots, then scrub them thoroughly.
2 Peel the lemons and oranges.
3 Slice the brown skin from the ginger.
4 If you have a juicer, put all the ingredients inside, then press. If you do not have a juicer but are using a blender, puree the ingredients until smooth, then pour the liquid through a strainer placed over a bowl to remove the last of the pulp. If you do not have any electric gadgets, turn to page 11 for help.
5 Serve over ice.

A perfect wake-me-up or pick-me-up!

CHEF'S TIP

For an even fresher taste, add three sprigs of fresh mint to the blend.

13

MELON MIXER

This refreshing juice is perfect for summer afternoons.

You Will Need
1 large honeydew melon
1 cucumber
1 lime
Ice to serve

Instructions
1 Halve the melon by slicing downward onto a chopping board with a large knife. Scrape out the seeds. Cut each half into quarters, then very carefully slice the melon flesh away from its hard rind. Chop the flesh into smaller chunks.
2 Wash the cucumber thoroughly, then trim off the ends.
3 Peel the lime.
4 If you have a juicer, put all the ingredients in the machine, then press. If you are using a blender, blend the ingredients until smooth, then pour the liquid through a strainer placed over a bowl to remove the pulp. If you do not have any electric gadgets, turn to page 11.
5 Pour into glasses, add ice—and enjoy!

Green and good for you!

CHEF'S TIP

Cucumber skin is where
most of the fiber and
vitamins are stored, so
leave it on when you juice.

limes

CHAPTER 3
SMOOTHIES AND SHAKES

Mix it up by adding smoothies and shakes to your drinks repertoire. Your friends will be lining up to try them.

What's So Smooth About Smoothies?

When you juice your produce, you strain out the pulp before drinking. With a smoothie, you just process your fruit and vegetables and drink it, pulp and all. That means smoothies are thicker and contain more healthy fiber than juices. Smoothies also often contain crushed ice and dairy products such as milk or yogurt. When you start adding ice cream to them, you should call them milkshakes.

The Lowdown on Shakes

A milkshake is a sweet, cold, frothy drink that contains milk, ice cream, and flavorings. This makes them higher in processed sugar and calories than smoothies and juices—but they make delicious treats.

Mastering the Basics
Milkshakes Without a Blender

Do not worry if you do not have a blender. You can still make milkshakes without one:

1 If you have a large container that seals tightly, like a mason jar or cocktail shaker, that would be ideal. If not, you will need a large bowl and a whisk—or just a fork and some patience.

2 Add ice cream, sorbet, or frozen yogurt, about ½ to ¾ cup (120–180 ml) per person. Then add about ¼ cup (60 ml) milk per person—or a non-dairy alternative such as almond milk.

3 Stir and mash your ice cream with a spoon or fork to break it up. If you are using a container, seal it, then shake for fifteen seconds. If you are working with a bowl, whisk until your shake is frothy.

4 Add any solid ingredients, such as candies or crumbled cookies.

Switch It Up

If you enjoy the Mango and Banana Smoothie on page 18, how about making mango lassi, a traditional Indian drink? Follow the same recipe, but leave out the banana. Rather than using 2 cups (480 ml) milk, use 1 cup (240 ml) milk and 1 cup (240 ml) natural yogurt. Flavor with 4 tsp honey and a pinch of ground cardamom. Delicious!

MANGO AND BANANA SMOOTHIE

Invite over three friends to share this sweet and creamy treat with you.

You Will Need
2 large mangoes
1 banana
2 cups (480 ml) low-fat milk
Handful of ice cubes
Sprigs of mint, to garnish

Instructions
1 Cut the "cheeks" off the mangoes, slicing on either side of the flat stone. Slice around the stones to remove as much flesh as possible. Carefully cut off the skin, then carve the flesh into chunks. Collect the running juice in a bowl.
2 Peel and slice the banana.
3 Put all the ingredients in a blender and puree until smooth.
4 Pour into glasses, garnish with a sprig of mint, and serve immediately.

A little taste of tropical paradise

CHEF'S TIP

For a dairy-free alternative, use soy milk or almond milk instead of cow's milk.

BLACK FOREST SHAKE

Inspired by German Black Forest gateau, these milkshakes are a step beyond delicious!

Decadent but totally divine!

You Will Need

3 cups (450 g) chocolate
   ice cream
1 cup (240 ml) milk
40 cocktail cherries
Dark chocolate, grated, to garnish

Instructions

1 Put the ice cream and milk
   in a blender, then pulse
   until combined.
2 Reserve eight to ten cherries.
   Add the rest of the cherries
   to the blender and process
   until smooth.
3 Pour the milkshake into four
   glasses, then garnish with the
   remaining cherries and grated
   dark chocolate.

CHEF'S TIP

If you do not like cherries,
switch in 1 cup (125 g)
of fresh raspberries.

CHAPTER 4
FRUIT

Many classic desserts are based on fruit, from cobblers and pies to fruit salads and stewed fruit. Choose your recipe, then choose your fruit!

Why Cook with Fruit?

Fruit is packed with fiber, minerals, and vitamin C, which all help to keep our digestive system, immune system, and the rest of the body in good shape. Fruit is ideal for dessert because it comforts our sweet tooth with naturally occurring sugar: fructose. The fructose in fruit is wrapped in fiber, which means we absorb it more slowly, avoiding the sugar rush we get from the processed sugar in candies and cookies. However, to avoid eating too much sugar, physicians recommend consuming no more than two servings of fruit per day.

How to Cook It

The simplest option is to serve fruit raw: sliced in a salad, mixed with yogurt, or topped with mascarpone. If you have more time, stew fruit in a saucepan with a little water or juice until soft. To bake fruit such as peaches or pears, halve or quarter them, then place in an ovenproof dish, flesh side up. Dot with a little unsalted butter and a sprinkle of brown sugar. Bake at 350°F (180°C) for eight to ten minutes.

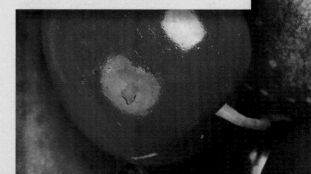

Mastering the Basics
Cobbler Dough

The recipe on the next page is for blueberry cobbler, but once you have mastered making cobbler dough, you can make any type of cobbler you like. Here is how to make enough dough for a four- to six-person cobbler:

1. In a mixing bowl, whisk together 1 egg, 5 tbsp sugar, and 4 tbsp milk.
2. Sift in ¾ cup (100 g) all-purpose flour, ½ tsp baking powder, and a pinch of salt. Stir thoroughly.
3. Melt 1 oz (30 g) of butter in a saucepan over a medium heat, then stir into the dough.
4. Finish off by mixing in ½ tsp vanilla extract.

blueberry crumble

Switch It Up

The blueberry cobbler on page 24 is an American classic. Want to surprise your friends by giving it a British twist? Follow the recipe exactly, but switch the cobbler dough for a "crumble" topping. Make this by rubbing together (using your fingers) ¾ cup (100 g) all-purpose flour, ¼ cup (50 g) softened butter, and ¼ cup (50 g) demerara sugar. When you have a breadcrumb texture, sprinkle the crumble over the blueberries, then bake. A crumble is usually served with custard.

BLUEBERRY COBBLER

This straightforward recipe serves up a comforting classic!

You Will Need

Cobbler dough to serve four to six
people (see the recipe on page 23)
4 cups (400 g) fresh blueberries
3 tbsp sugar
5 tbsp orange juice

Instructions

1 Preheat your oven to 370°F (190°C).
2 Prepare your cobbler dough by
following the recipe on page 23.
Set to one side.
3 In a baking dish, combine the
blueberries, sugar, and orange juice.
4 Spoon the dough over the fruit.
To get the cobbled effect, flick the
balls of dough fairly randomly.
5 Bake for thirty to forty minutes, until
the topping is golden and the fruit
is bubbling.

blueberries

Serve your cobbler with a
scoop of vanilla ice cream.

CHEF'S TIP

Switch your blueberries for
blackberries and raspberries,
or sliced peaches and apricots.

PEACH MELBA

This famous dessert was invented in the nineteenth century to honor Australian opera singer Dame Nellie Melba.

You Will Need
2 cups (480 ml) water
2 cups (400 g) sugar
Juice of ½ lemon
4 peaches
1½ cups (190 g) raspberries
2 tbsp confectioners' sugar
4 scoops vanilla ice cream

Instructions
1 Put the water, sugar, and lemon juice in a large saucepan.
2 Heat gently while the sugar dissolves, then bring the liquid to the boil. Turn down the heat to let the syrup simmer for five minutes.
3 In the meantime, cut the peaches in half and remove the pits.
4 Place the peach halves in the syrup. Cook for three minutes, then turn them over and cook for another three minutes. Check the peaches are tender by prodding them with a fork. When tender, remove from the pan and leave to cool.
5 Put the raspberries and confectioners' sugar in a blender and process until smooth. Then press your raspberry sauce through a strainer to remove seeds.
6 Using your fingers, peel the skins from the cooled peaches.
7 Place two peach halves and one scoop of ice cream in each bowl. Drizzle with raspberry sauce.

A perfect balance of sweet and tart!

CHEF'S TIP

To give a richer flavor to the peaches, add 1 tsp of vanilla extract to the sugar syrup.

CHAPTER 5

CAKES AND BAKED GOODS

Baking is fun to do—and creates results that taste fantastic and have a definite wow factor.

Know Your Ingredients

Flour is the base ingredient for all baked goods: it provides the framework for the cake. Sugar adds sweetness and plays a role in the chemical reactions that happen during baking. Sugar helps baked goods turn golden, and helps the flour form strong strands of gluten when it is combined with moisture and heat. Fat, in the form of butter, margarine, shortening, or oil, adds moistness and softness. Eggs add structure and texture. A liquid, such as buttermilk, milk, or juice, helps blend the mixture and hold it together.

Going Up

All baked goods need a leavening agent to make them rise. Baking powder and baking soda are used for cakes, while yeast is used for breads. When combined with the other ingredients, these leavening agents produce carbon dioxide, which creates a fluffy texture in the finished baked products.

Mastering the Basics
Knowing When a Cake Is Done

No one wants to eat a cake that has overcooked its way to being dried out and crumbly. A cake that is still raw in the middle is even worse! Try these tests to check if your oven-baked cake is ready. For all methods, remove the cake from the oven, using oven mitts, before testing. Only test toward the end of the cooking time, because repeated opening of the oven door will make your cake sink.

1 Insert a toothpick or skewer in the center of the cake. If it comes out clean (apart from one or two crumbs), your cake is cooked through. The exception is recipes like the brownies on page 30, which are meant to be deliciously fudgy in the middle.

2 The center of the cake should feel springy when you gently press on it. Remember that the cake is hot, so perform this maneuver swiftly!

3 If the edges of the cake have dried out and are starting to pull away from the pan, it is done!

Switch It Up

If you enjoy the Apple Cake on page 32, it is easy to customize the recipe. Try swapping the apples for the same quantity of pears. Another alternative is to switch the fresh fruit for ¾ cup (110 g) dried fruit, such as raisins and cherries. Or, for something a little less healthy, go for ¾ cup (130 g) chocolate chips.

29

BROWNIES

This recipe makes ten brownies, so make sure you invite friends to share!

You Will Need
4 oz (110 g) butter, plus extra for greasing
1 cup (200 g) super-fine sugar
¼ cup (30 g) cocoa powder
½ tsp vanilla extract
2 medium eggs, beaten
1 cup (120 g) all-purpose flour
¼ tsp baking powder
¼ tsp salt

Instructions
1 Preheat the oven to 350°F (180°C).
2 Using a little butter, lightly grease the insides of a roughly 8 inch (20 cm) square baking pan.
3 Melt the butter in a saucepan over a low heat, then pour it into a large mixing bowl.
4 Add the sugar, cocoa powder, vanilla extract, and eggs. Stir thoroughly.
5 Sift in the flour, then add the baking powder and salt. Mix well before spooning into the baking pan.
6 Bake for around twenty-five minutes, until the outside is crisp but the inside is still a little gooey.
7 Slice and serve!

These are everybody's favorite!

cocoa powder

CHEF'S TIP

Try adding ¼ cup (40 g) of chopped peanuts, walnuts, pecans, or almonds to your brownie mix.

APPLE CAKE

This one is old-fashioned but always a winner!

Give your loaf a dust of confectioners' sugar.

You Will Need

4 oz (115 g) butter, plus extra for greasing
$^7/_8$ cup (175 g) super-fine sugar
2 large eggs
$^1/_2$ cup (120 ml) buttermilk
1 tsp vanilla extract
2 cups (240 g) all-purpose flour
1$^1/_2$ tsp baking powder
3 medium apples

Instructions

1. Preheat the oven to 350°F (180°C).
2. Grease a loaf pan or a similarly sized rectangular baking pan.
3. Melt the butter in a saucepan over a low heat.
4. Whisk together the sugar and eggs until they look foamy.
5. In a large bowl, mix the sugar and eggs together with the melted butter, buttermilk, and vanilla extract.
6. Sift in the flour, then add the baking powder. Mix thoroughly to combine.
7. Peel the apples, cut into quarters, remove the cores, and slice. Stir the apples into the mixture.
8. Pour the mixture into the loaf pan, then bake for around fifty minutes until golden brown.

CHEF'S TIP

For a spicier flavor, switch the vanilla extract for ¼ tsp of ground cinnamon.

33

CHAPTER 6
MINI DESSERTS

Mini desserts look cute and enticing! Going small means you can mix and match your desserts, without your friends feeling too full.

How to Go Small

You can miniaturize any nonbaked dessert simply by cutting it in tiny slices, forming it inside a cookie mold rather than a baking pan, or serving it in a cup or spoon rather than a bowl. Turn to page 38 to find out how to make mini cheesecakes by miniaturizing in this way.

When you are baking mini desserts, you usually need to reduce the cooking time if you are working from a full-size recipe. Keep checking your desserts during baking to make sure they do not burn.

Switch It Up

Once you have mastered a classic like meringue, it would be a shame not to use the skill again and again! How about creating the British classic Eton mess? Just throw chunks and crumbles from four meringue nests into four glasses or bowls. Whip 2 cups (480 ml) heavy cream and spoon it into the glasses. Chop about 20 fresh stawberries, then mix in with the rest of the mess. Chill before serving.

Mastering the Basics
Meringues

The Mini Pavlovas recipe on page 36 calls for mini meringues. You can buy ready-made meringues in some bakeries, grocery stores, and large supermarkets. You can also buy meringue powder to save yourself time.

Or you can make meringues yourself! Here is how to make eight to twelve mini meringues:

1 Preheat the oven to 300°F (150°C).
2 Cover two baking trays with parchment paper (baking paper).
3 Separate 4 large egg whites from their yolks by passing the cracked eggs between your palms, letting the whites drip into a clean bowl and keeping gentle hold of the yolks. Discard the yolks or keep for omelets.
4 Using an electric mixer, whisk the egg whites until they form soft peaks. You can do this by hand but it will take a very long time.
5 Gradually add $1\frac{1}{8}$ cup (225 g) super-fine sugar, whisking after adding each spoonful.
6 Whisk until the mixture is thick and shiny, which will take about five minutes with an electric mixer.
7 For each meringue, spoon one heaped tablespoon of the mixture onto a baking tray, then gently smooth into a disk shape, pressing the center with the back of a spoon to make a dent (to hold the filling later).
8 Bake for twenty to twenty-five minutes until the meringues are crisp, then turn off the oven, open the door, and—leaving the trays in the oven—leave to cool gradually to room temperature.

MINI PAVLOVAS

These are mini versions of the meringue dessert named for ballerina Anna Pavlova in the 1920s.

You Will Need

8–12 mini meringue nests (see page 35)
1½ cups (360 ml) heavy cream
1 cup (125 g) raspberries
1 cup (125 g) blueberries
Confectioners' sugar to dust
2 sprigs of fresh mint

Instructions

1 Make or buy meringue nests.
2 Whip the heavy cream until soft peaks form.
3 Spoon the cream into the hollow in the center of each nest.
4 Arrange the fruit on each nest so it looks pretty.
5 Sprinkle with a little confectioners' sugar and garnish with mint leaves.

These look too pretty to eat!

CHEF'S TIP

Try mixing your berries with 2 tbsp of jelly, then leave out the confectioners' sugar.

MINI CHEESECAKES

Make twelve of these little cheesecakes—
they look and taste gorgeous!

graham cracker crumbs

You Will Need
5 oz (140 g) graham crackers
2 oz (55 g) butter
2 lemons
14 oz (400 g) cream cheese
6 tbsp confectioners' sugar
2 tbsp heavy cream
1 lime, sliced

Instructions
1 In a small saucepan, melt the butter over a low heat.
2 Put the graham crackers in a zip-top bag and crush them.
3 Mix together the cracker crumbs and melted butter,
   then press into twelve cookie molds—or a full-size
   rectangular baking pan if you are going to cut your
   cheesecake into mini portions later.
4 Lightly grate the lemon skin to collect the zest (outer peel),
   then cut the lemons in half and squeeze them for their juice.
5 In a large bowl, mix the lemon juice and zest with the
   cream cheese, sugar, and cream. Use a folding motion
   to introduce air into the mixture.
6 Spoon the cream cheese mixture over your base or bases,
   then chill in the refrigerator for at least half an hour.
7 Ease your mini cheesecakes out of their molds. If you used a large
   pan, carefully remove your cake, then cut into twelve portions.
8 Garnish with slices of lime.

Fancy enough for a restaurant!

CHEF'S TIP

If you use a large baking pan, make sure you line it with parchment paper so you can slide out your cheesecake easily.

CHAPTER 7

FROZEN YOGURT

Frozen yogurt—or froyo—is a lower-fat and slightly sourer-tasting alternative to ice cream. It is perfect to share on a summer afternoon.

Do It Yourself

There is probably a frozen yogurt place down the road, so why make your own? The homemade variety comes at a fraction of the price, and with no trace of stabilizers and thickeners. There is no store-bought flavor that you cannot create at home with a little time and know-how: try sugar sprinkles or crunchy oats, whole or pureed fruit, or honey and a squeeze of lemon.

Is It Healthy?

Frozen yogurt is a dairy dessert like ice cream, but it is made with yogurt rather than milk and cream, which means it contains a lot less fat, even if made with full-fat Greek yogurt. Homemade froyo might have less sugar than some store-bought varieties, but it still has plenty, so be sure to share your desserts. For a slightly healthier option, switch processed sugar for a few tablespoons of honey—taste as you mix to check on the sweetness.

Switch It Up

Once you have mastered a basic frozen yogurt (see opposite), you can add any ingredients you like. Stir in 1 tsp vanilla extract and ¾ cup (130 g) chocolate chips to make vanilla chocolate chip froyo. Or melt the chips by placing them in a bowl over a pan of simmering water, then add to the yogurt during blending.

Mastering the Basics
Frozen Yogurt

If you put yogurt straight in the freezer, it will set hard as a brick. The first step to make fluffy frozen yogurt is to add sugar before freezing. The sugar molecules get in the way of the growing ice crystals, creating a lighter texture. The second step is to whisk your yogurt before and during freezing. Here is how to make around 4 cups (960 ml) of plain frozen yogurt.

1 You will need 4 cups (960 ml) of your chosen yogurt. Go for low-fat plain yogurt for a healthier version, or full-fat Greek yogurt for a creamier taste.

2 Add 1 cup (200 g) super-fine sugar to the yogurt.

3 Using an electric blender or a whisk, mix until combined and airy.

4 Spoon the mix into a clean, freezer-safe box with a lid.

5 Freeze the yogurt for sixty to ninety minutes, until it is beginning to solidify, then beat with a whisk or fork to break up solid chunks. Repeat the whisking every ninety minutes, but leave the yogurt to set undisturbed for at least one hour before serving. It will take about six hours for your yogurt to freeze fully.

6 Your yogurt will keep for up to two months in the freezer.

MINT AND CHOC POPS

Depending on the size of your molds, this recipe will make six to eight pops.

You Will Need
4 cups (960 ml) plain yogurt
1 cup (200 g) super-fine sugar
1 tsp peppermint extract
¾ cup (130 g) chocolate chips
Drop of green food coloring (optional)

Instructions
1 Put your yogurt, sugar, and peppermint extract in a blender or large mixing bowl.
2 Using a blender or hand-held whisk, blend until smooth.
3 Using a spoon, stir through the chocolate chips.
4 To give a green tint, add a drop or two of food coloring. Most food colorings are made from artificial ingredients, so leave out this step if you prefer.
5 Spoon the mixture into ice-pop molds, then freeze for four to six hours, until solid.

chocolate chips

The perfect balance of fresh and creamy!

CHEF'S TIP

Switch the peppermint extract for
2 tbsp of chopped fresh mint leaves,
which have the benefit of tinting
your yogurt slightly green without
using coloring.

VERY BERRY

Choose your favorite berries for this quick but delectable dessert.

Better than anything you can buy at the store!

You Will Need

4 cups (960 ml) plain yogurt
1 cup (200 g) super-fine sugar
1 cup (125 g) frozen berries, such as cranberries or blueberries

Instructions

1 If you want the yogurt to be pink and smooth, thaw the berries, then puree them in a blender. If you want to keep the fruit whole, go straight to step 2.
2 Put the yogurt and sugar in a blender or large mixing bowl. Using an electric blender or a whisk, mix until smooth.
3 Using a spoon, stir through the pureed or whole fruit.
4 Pour the mix into a clean, freezer-safe box with a lid.
5 Freeze for four to six hours, stirring after ninety minutes, then again after three hours, to keep the texture fluffy.

plain yogurt

CHEF'S TIP

To create swirls of pink and white, do not completely mix through the pureed fruit in step 3.

GLOSSARY

baking powder A leavening agent that creates bubbles of carbon dioxide gas when combined with heat and moisture.

boil When a liquid is so hot that it releases large bubbles of gas.

calories Units used to measure the energy value of food.

cardamom Seeds of a plant in the ginger family.

cinnamon A spice made from the bark of a Southeast Asian tree.

fiber Long molecules that are contained in plants and help with digestion.

gluten A mixture of two proteins found in cereal grains such as wheat, barley, rye, and some oats.

intolerances Inabilities to eat a food without having side effects.

juices Strained liquids extracted from fruits and vegetables.

leavening agents Baking powder, baking soda, and yeast, which are added to baked goods to make them rise and develop a light texture in the oven.

nutrient Substance found in food that provides essential nourishment for health and growth.

protein A substance found in lentils, beans, nuts, seeds, meat, fish, eggs, and dairy products that is essential for growth and health.

saturated fat A type of "unhealthy" fat that is usually found in animal products such as meat and dairy.

simmer To be at a temperature hot enough to bubble gently but not to boil.

smoothies Thick drinks made from pureed fruits and vegetables.

stewed Cooked slowly in liquid.

vanilla extract A liquid vanilla flavoring obtained from vanilla beans.

vegan A person who does not eat any animal products, including eggs, milk products, and honey.

whisking Stirring or beating ingredients using the quick movement of a wire utensil.

whole grains Grains obtained from cereal crops, such as wheat, that have not had their germ (kernel) and bran (outer layer) removed.

yeast A microscopic fungus used to make bread rise.

FURTHER READING

Books

Harroun, Deborah. *Best 100 Smoothies for Kids*. Boston, MA: Harvard Common Press, 2015.

Huff, Lisa. *Kid Chef Bakes*. Emeryville, CA: Rockridge Press, 2017.

Owen, Ruth. *Kids Cook!* New York, NY: Windmill Books, 2017.

Polito, Clara. *Clara Cakes: Delicious and Simple Vegan Desserts for Everyone*. New York, NY: Powerhouse Books, 2017.

Websites

Become a Better Baker
www.becomeabetterbaker.com
Discover baking tips and techniques.

Cooking Tips and Resources
kidshealth.org/en/teens/whats-cooking.html
Read up on more tips to use in the kitchen.

Talking About Juice Safety: What You Need to Know
www.fda.gov/Food/ResourcesForYou/Consumers/ucm110526.htm
Find out more about making juice safely.

38 Fun Desserts for Teens to Make at Home
diyprojectsforteens.com/desserts-teens-to-make-at-home
Find links to fun dessert recipes.

INDEX